The Coventry Carol

Primo

Traditional
Arr. by Dennis Alexander

Secondo

Primo

Secondo
42
f
mp
47
mf
52
57
mp
62
rit.
p